Wunderkammer

Wunderkammer

Poems by

Matthew James Friday

Cover design by Shay Culligan
Cover image by Maria Teneva on Unsplash

ISBN: 979-8-90146-811-1
Library of Congress Control Number: 2026935116

Kelsay Books
502 South 1040 East, A-119
American Fork, Utah 84003
Kelsaybooks.com

*This book is dedicated to my wife, Jill,
and daughter, Leni-Grace—
the greatest wonders of them all.*

Acknowledgments

Poems from this collection have been published in the following journals and awarded the following prizes:

Borderless: "The Poet, God," "The Star of the Forest," "Sunflower"
Burningword Literary Journal: "A Steiner Piano Shop," "Three First-Grade Boys on the Titanic"
Cordite Poetry Review: "Cleaning Caravans"
Dawntreader: "Elegy for a Brandon Oyster," "How the Hummingbird Came to Be," "Gokotta," Memory of Spirit," "The Patience of Trees," "The Song of the Pink Dogwood Tree," "Whale Blessing," "Why Not the Cherry Tree"
Feed the Holy/Masticadores USA: "The Grapes," "On New Year's Eve"
Ginosko Literary Review: "Different River," "Dishwasher Revelation," "Flying Kites in Namche Bazaar, Nepal"
Heather Feather Review: "Why Not the Cherry Tree"
Inlandia: A Literary Journey: "Getting Gas in Roseburg, Oregon," "Skunk Dying"
Lothlorien Poetry Journal: Various Haiku
Lunch Ticket: "The Wisdom of Photons"
Main Street Rag: "Dear Life"
The Odd Magazine: "The Golden Crowned Kinglet," "A Prayer for a Certain Type of Truck Driver"
Oregon English Journal: "Elegy for the Caught Fish," "Free Refills," "Ode to Joy," "Snow Tornado," "TikTok Lockdown," "Witness"
Oregon Poetry Association's 2024 Prose Poem Competition: "The Rose" (Honorary Mention)
Panoplyzine: "Prospects of a Young Hawk"
Qutub Minar Review: "Secrets"

Saving Ourselves Anthology: "Beyond the Mail," "Objection"
The Schuylkill Valley Journal: "A Bottle Longs to Be Reunited with its Owner"
Shot Glass Journal: "Calculating the Cost"
Sparks of Calliope: "Fishing for Poems"
Tipton Poetry Journal: "The Vastness"
The Trouvaille Review: "How the Hummingbird Came to Be"
Verbal Art: Various Haiku, "Elegy for the Caught Fish," "Pine Eagle"
Weber—The Contemporary West: "Ukiyo-e in Oregon"
The Source (Bend, OR) Newspaper, 2025 Poetry Contest: "Unenforceable" (2nd Place)

Additionally, the following poems appeared in *Origami Poems Project* microchaps:

River Songs: "4 Otters in the Metolius River," "Deschutes Circles," "On Hearing 'River Snow by Liu Zongyuan Recited in Chinese," "The River Reclaimed," "The Whirlpool"
The Oregon Sonnets (microchap): "At Belknap Hot Springs," "At the Beach," "Mother-in-Law Versus Bear," "Running Oregon," "The Song of Night," "Transient Moon"
The Wunderkammer: "The Bat," "Courting Eagles," "Elegy for a Bandon Oyster," "His Wings," "Hope in January," "Pine Eagle"

Special thanks to Becca Reynolds at Deschutes Public Library for giving me opportunities to share my poetry with the public via readings and writing workshops. To Ellen, Carol, Melissa, Jane and Sandy of Skyhooks—my poetry critique group—for their excellent feedback and editorial advice.

Contents

About Wunderkammer

I. NATURALIA

American Kestrel 19
Gokotta 20
Elegy for the Bandon Oyster 21
His Wings 22
The Golden Crowned Kinglet 23
Pine Eagle 24
The Patience of Trees 25
Songs from the Douglas Fir 26
Courting Eagles 29
Memory of Spirit 30
The River Reclaimed 31
4 Otters in the Metolius River 32
Shared Language 33
Six Brown Pelicans 34
Prospects of a Young Hawk 35
Secrets 36
The Black-Beaked God 37
The End of September 38
Rock chucks 39
At the Beach 40
The Mourning Doves 41
On New Year's Eve 42
The Bat 43
Fishing for Poems 44
Haiku 46

II. EXOTICA

How the Hummingbird Came to Be 49
Why Not the Cherry Tree 50
The Star of the Forest 51
The Whirlpool 52
Rabbit, Being 53
The Song of Night 54
The Vastness 55
On Hearing 'River Snow' by Liu Zongyuan
Recited in Chinese 56
Deschutes' Circles 57
Ukiyo-e in Oregon 58
Skunk Dying 59
The Horned Owl Gathers 60
Hummingbird Versus Cat 61
Song for Decaying Angler Fish 62
The Gray Whale 63
Whale Blessing 65
The Owl 66
After the Open-Mic Reading 67
For All the Alligators 68
What Children Already Know 72
The Song of a Pink Dogwood Tree 73
The Salmon Bake 74
In Yellowjacket Heaven 76
Flying Kites at Namche Bazaar, Nepal 77
The Snow Tornado 78

III. ARTIFICIALIA

In My Life 81
Looking Down 82
An Osprey and a Traffic Circle 84
A Bottle Longs to Be Reunited with Its Owner 85
A Traffic Circle in Bend, OR 87
Getting Gas in Roseburg, OR 88
Wisdom Versus Experience 89
Skeleton Doll 90
The Grapes 91
Small World, Skyler 92
The Pack 93
Transient Moon 94
Three First-Grade Boys on the Titanic 95
A Steiner Piano Shop 96
Long Way 97
Prayer for a Certain Type of Truck Driver 98
Free Refills 99
Cleaning Caravans 100
Beyond the Mail 101
The Springs 102
Dear Life 103
Half 104
TikTok Lockdown 106
Between 108
Haiku 110

IV. SCIENTIFICA

The Poet, God 113
Ode to Joy 114
The Box 115
The Under 116
The Rose 118
Cape Kiwanda 119
Unenforceable 120
Calculating the Cost 121
Elegy for the Caught Fish 122
Hope in January 124
The Wisdom of Photons 125
Of Love and Atoms 126
Different River 127
This Earth Day 128
Objection 129
Mother-in-Law Versus Fate 130
Running Across Oregon 131
Sunflower 132
Dishwasher Revelation 133
Witness 134
Cicada Concert in Lucca 135
Song from 'Landscape in the Riesengebirge,'
by C.D. Friedrich 136
At Belknap Hot Springs 137
Return to Trees 138
Haiku 139

Notes 141
Postscript 143

About Wunderkammer

Originating in the royal households of Europe over four hundred years ago, the Wunderkammer (German) or Cabinet/Room of Curiosities, was a collection of highly valuable and fascinating items.

Over the centuries, the concept took on a more scientific, humanistic approach, evolving from displays of regal wealth to proto-museums that displayed items that stimulated curiosity and wonder.

There were numerous ways to organize a Wunderkammer, but the four basic components were:

Naturalia—Nature and natural phenomena

Exotica—the exotic or out of the ordinary

Artificialia—artificial, constructed

Scientifica—relating to a scientific principle

To learn more, go to:
www.dailyartmagazine.com/cabinets-of-curiosities

I.
NATURALIA

American Kestrel

Face to face
you are smaller than your shadow's quiver.

You let your legend do the aiming.

You perch on the riparian bush,
on the edge of a searching hunger,
breast flecked with the brown prints
of a dirty patterning thumb on dough.

I could cup you in my hands,
or offer you as a prayer, send
you flying heavenwards or squeeze
until I feel Biblical, but

I fear those claws
would teach me too many lessons.

You arrow away
before I offer you permission,
and I am left bereft
and learning.

Gokotta

Gokotta (Swedish): the act of waking up early with the purpose of going outside to listen to the first birds sing.

Living in the high desert is the excuse.
Drawn-out droughts and wingless winters.

My heart aches for the birdsong's unspooling
of time's quickly wound-up wound. In Bend

I make-do with the blackbird's reedy trill,
a cooing morning dove, the sparrow gossip,

anything to be boy again, to be blessed by
the ancient inspiration to chisel holes in bone.

But in these slow-burning End of Days
wildfires reroute migrants, billions fall under

cat spells or the trick of windowpanes,
eggs hatch too early, spring begins thinner,

we replace forests with poultry farms,
and canaries of all colors cry out.

If only we would wake up early enough.

Elegy for the Bandon Oyster

I watch the man stab and crank
your shell open, shucking your gash
apart with quick flicks of the wrist,
exposing your mucous mystery
to an explanation of gore, denying
the magical workings of innards.

I am sorry it's not harder work.
You deserve sweat, swearing, break-
ages. He cleans your homely shell
halves, two sedimentary marvels,
encrusted by salt's solidifying efforts
and the colossal miracle of water.
You're tossed in a basket, clinking
with all the other culinary victims.

His Wings

Fresh out of the day's forgetting,
we find him full of summoning
from atop a ponderosa pine tree,
a whisper of color in the hastening

heat-death of December evening.
We turn our backs on Brookswood
Boulevard where commuters risk icy
tire-spins to watch his Islamic moon

body, head arced towards us, nodding
as if he's the one God guiding us
across the desert. When he leaps
into the darkness, we gasp at His

wings as wide as ignorance. He forgets
us, and we continue along our path.

The Golden Crowned Kinglet

Today I want to be like you
wearing the sun on my head
and bars of gold in sudden wings.

I want to shatter the moment
flitting from branch to branch,
pausing to become a tiny Buddha
before being busy again. Seeing me

you curve so sharply away
like a meteor avoiding the Earth.
You always know what's best for you.

Pine Eagle

I saw you, white wave constellation
rising above the Deschutes River,
chasing out a crow from your current.

I sat by a Milky Way of ruined rocks
and the upturned ocean of the sky,
and you spilled upstream, rapid

and uneven, as if debating ownership
with the river, orbiting pine trees to
prove to Odin that you can see all.

The Patience of Trees

We accuse trees
of losing their leaves,
but we don't credit them
with their patience.

We who cannot stand
to misplace a phone
or wait in line
for a needle to drop.

So finely tuned
to the sun's long touch,
they sleep naked,
trusting in the return.

We who do not trust
our neighbors to agree,
when to rest a gun,
when to distrust words.

Where do they go
during the bare months?
What woody dreams
satisfy so much sap?

Songs from the Douglas Fir

I

Wake up in the middle of the night
to their hushing lullabies, protective
boughs of parental grain, still

silhouettes of Titans keeping Sky
at bay, rarely swayed by Zeus'
most jealous bolts and blasts.

Mature, they turn suburb mansions
into doll houses, toy towns spreading
fungus on their roots. They reach up,

aiding Atlas in his efforts to keep
the West from tilting into the Pacific.
In decades they advise us to drop

deciduous stresses. The only work
of worth is to build rings, ignore
the neighbors, know that growth

is its own slow reward, that a seed
as small as a baby's nail can grow
giants other trees make myths about.

II

In those days of axing disbelief
one Douglas was measured 100m taller
than Liberty, higher than redwoods.
Now a 1000 years of old growth all gone,
except for a few giants in Olympic Park,
forgotten fortresses in logged Oregon
that gift unique habitats and store
carbon uncountable until they become
cross-sections kept in old photographs,
arboretums for children to lose
count of the rings.

III

Out of the cone sticks is a three-pointed bract shaped like the hind legs and tail of a mouse. This gave shape to a Native story of how Mouse needed saving during a forest fire. Maple Tree and Western Cedar refused, unable to resist the fire themselves. Only Douglas Fir's bark offered that protection. Mouse climbed into the cone just in time.

IV

Oregon Pine/Yew-leafed-fir/
False Hemlock (*Pseudotsuga menziesii*)
Douglas Spruce/ Douglas Fir.

Named after David Douglas, botanist
from Scotland, Northwest explorer,
early European mountaineer, importer

of pines and plants to transform Britain
and Europe. 1834 he died in Hawaii,
falling into a pit trap, mauled by a bull

and possibly robbed by an escaped
convict and bullock hunter—coincidence?
Ask the firs and they will confirm.

He rises resurrected with every trunk.

Courting Eagles

A pair of bald eagles yin & yang
the early evening blue, a cluster

of clouds heaping the background
behind the doubled-over daub

of a half winking moon. They spiral
like two excited galaxies, never

colliding, just courting, rising,
blurring into the hint of heavens.

Memory of Spirit

Let there be wisdom
in a sudden sight of you
white head and tail undeniable
wings in time to the Columbia's current
you are level with us on the road
turned into fish tails and carrion
words of this poem
and a memory
of spirit

The River Reclaimed

The geese have reclaimed their river.
They hold court on their current,
gathered in hundreds, mimicking
the summer floats that crowded
their water with that bloated sense
of ownership, drinks and indifference
to the river's true purpose. Tourists
a long-diluted rumor, leaving geese
to feed, upturned white exclamations
stating the points of reclamation.

4 Otters in the Metolius River

Out of the water they snap,
four glistening ligaments
contracting a fallen trunk.

Back into the water they crash
and undulate upstream, up
the arm of the river, resurfacing

a remembrance of muscles,
constricting in questions
answered further upstream.

The riverbank always beckons
otter again. 'Otter' too easy
a word for one so aligned

with the current, the earth
brown body of the world,
the giggles of children.

Shared Language

After three years of watching the river,

I see a snouting log spearing downstream,
back-end oaring the water. Beaver . . .?
I run back along the bank to watch
the line of bubbles reproduce proof.

My one-year-old hangs from my wife's back,
arms outstretched in a crucifix of fatigue,
seeing evening darken for the first time.
Father, why have you forsaken me?

A beaver calmly awakening my faith.
I direct a strolling Spanish-speaking family
and we collect on the riparian fringe.
My wife and child resurrect a second

beaver, sitting calmly crunching thin
driftwood. This beaver comes within
arm's length and ducks underwater,
into a bank, gone before the Spanish-

speaking family can find proof. I show
photos. They point to a coiling body.
An otter has joined the syntax of surprise.
We congratulate each other with smiles,

nods, a shared language rooted in water.

Six Brown Pelicans

mimicking the Big Dipper,
with wings of constant waves
and rolling doughy clouds

they break apart, into pairs,
each an inseparable Gemini
looking for a fortune in fish.

An hour later, they reunite,
a constellation of kite-stiff
wings and pterosaur heads,

dipping
bills into the infinite
green-dark waving hunger
of being.

Prospects of a Young Hawk

Finding a stumbling short cut from a brewery
along Highway 97

we are shuddered to a stop
by a juvenile red-tailed hawk on the fence

looking at us, no, through us, huge
in our ignorance,
calm in its claws.

Further up the path, lay spewed
the contents of a life from the flapping mouth of a tent,

and in the months ahead
the path will sprawl with tents and the sodden stories
of a civilization unable to care for itself . . .

and the young hawk
will leave.

Secrets

Across the river trail path
the striped whipsnake s's
its secret: of all the moments

to be revealed, I am chosen,
brakes tightening, suspension
rearing. I watch the snake

spell out its exposure
and slip into the riparian
relief just as an oblivious

cyclist slices past. Seconds
earlier, the wheels would have
silenced all secrets. Shhssss.

The Black-Beaked God

The parents rake the suddenly absent air,
crying for the black-beaked god to intervene.

Under the pines

the kind lady from a local animal sanctuary
tends to the stricken fledgling, feeling
for fractures, explanations for the staggering,
drunken sloop, juvenile wings smattering,
legs projecting near-death claws. She sweeps
the swooning child towards a cardboard box,
makes calls, takes pictures, seeks advice from local
officials as needles and torn twigs spear down—
just parents trying to save a child with a fury
any mammal would comprehend. The fledgling
lollops around, wings cracking, sitting back
on its splayed tail feathers like a drunk reeling
from a fight. The kind lady cups the raven's
panic like a prayer so it can stomach the box.
The kind lady stands back, worried. Avian flu.

"You think I should wring its neck?"
She thinks better, leaves it in the box.

The next day, under the pines,
nothing.

No box, no baby, not heartache with wings.

Just the black-beaked god wondering
what all the fuss was.

The End of September

is when
you realize
the swallows
have gone

like the unimaginably vast
space
in atoms
between a nucleus
and unpredictable
electrons

all you see
is the empti
ness
in the air
between
what was
and what is

You

Rock chucks

sun-bath on stoney patios, watching
a queue of cars tailback, blocking
their once million-dollar views
of Deschutes River and the Cascades,
not that they care: grass to eat, cheat
the red-tailed hawk, a willing mate
in spring, fur to insulate the winter.
Ignorant to what smoky skies mean,
they don't understand any statistics.
Dismiss them all with a wave of a paw.
Keep the sprinklers working, the grass
green, the little ones room enough
to scamper about. Their votes go
to keeping coyote on his many toes.

At the Beach

Middle aged eyes see sands scattered
with entropy: the empty fate of crabs,
wriggled trails of kelp, tree-toys of
tantrumming storms, the frothy frown
of waves patrolled by crows and gulls,
scything the scud with bill and claws.

Then I hear the children playing,
forcing the surf to smile, and being
Brahma and Shiva with sandcastles,
the Buddha dogs barking, absorbed
in the stick and the chase of being,
an artist raking a yin-yang symbol,

all the troughs and peaks of fate
soiled by the plastic litter we create.

The Mourning Doves

Confusion or adaptation causes
the male mourning dove to use
the 45 degree angled gutter pipe
as a place to coo, coo, coo. Seconds
later its mate clatters the gutter.

He turns to keep a black star bead
on me while facing washed-out
green wooden panels and H.O.A
hemmed green linings where once
he would have wooed with leaves.

He keeps cooing until the gutter
empties. He sputters after his loss.

On New Year's Eve

the unexpected sun lubricates
the solidified landscape, accompanied
by dripping, dripping.

A green bush exhales
two sudden surges of whiteness:

one of the Ten Thousand Forms
last chance to be more.

The first column merges
with the second,
heaping into itself like faint dough.

A few gusts of chilled wind
scatter the flecks of mating energy.
They rally, weakened,

growing few, tracking the sun's gift
along the wooden walkway, forming
squabbling groups, pairs,

all hoping in that frenzied fly way
that no bird sees them. How envious

I am of their New Year's Eve,
of them living poetry rather than writing it.

The Bat

When asked to explain what a poem is, I say

a bat

that most successful of all mammals,
drawing up the string of the evening,
circumferencing the Douglas fir's column
that reaches right up to that first star

blamed

for disease and world plague

a metaphor for who we are.

Fishing for Poems

I was asked, what is poetry like?

Perhaps like the northern flicker
riffling the rim of the path, probing
into the wood-chipped, damp earth
for a morsel to maintain its spirit.

No, it's like fishing.

You set up your intentions
on the bank of the brown page
and cast off into the current
of images and ideas.
Then wait
for inspiration
to nibble your bait, sink
the float and the poem bites.

Now the real struggle begins:
wrestling with imagery, trying
to land the wriggling language
on the bank of verses.

Out of the plopping water
flops the first draft. Disappointingly
underdeveloped.

Poets never exaggerate the catch.
A poem is always ‘this’ big,
often smaller, a toddler

in the powerful play,
but still something to contribute
to Whitman’s waters.

Haiku

Proud kayak fisher
showing first lingcod catch.
Fish: no comment.

Under my foot
a molted crab shell crunches—
fortune cookies.

Struggling beetle
flip it back on its front—
many ways to love.

At the dead of night
two raccoons snort and forage—
Moon shows other worlds.

Woodpecker nails roof tiles,
man strums hard on his front porch—
annoying neighbors.

Osprey nest made with
multi-colored plastic shreds—
America's flag.

The cliff face sutra—
clumps of poppies and balsam
grow the hard way.

II.
EXOTICA

How the Hummingbird Came to Be

Something was missing from Creation.
Almost all extremes had been explored,
but imagination still conjured tricks.
So the Creator left a niche for Being to fill,
frantically on the edge of starvation, needing
to feed every two hours or die, so much
sugar to keep impossible wings beating,
cells racing on the edge of atomic function.
There needed to be just less than enough
flowers for desperate tongues to find
liquid sun. The Creator added aggression
so that not even miracles were spared.
For there to be diversity despite the mix
of impossible ingredients is the miracle.

Why Not the Cherry Tree

with its dark web of branches
offering galaxies of darkening orbs.

At Idiot's Grace Farm—Pick Your Own
my middle-school nephew proudly
conquers ladders and black hole branches
one star at a time. I stand below,

an Odin steadying the ladder,
belly-bucket layering with half-hearted
labors, one eye on him, the other
on cherries bouncing below.

We consume half the universe
in nuclear bursts of flavor,
ground littered with leaves
of teenage Loki's enthusiasm.

We go to weigh our efforts.
The orchard owners are dwarfed
by hidden hard work, preaching
picking etiquette, stained scales.

Clouds gather over the Columbia River.
We read the runes and return
to Midgard, WA, laden with treasure.

The Star of the Forest

Scientists are still finding
a few names on the secret roll-call
of those close to erasure.
Tiny panicking plants
in remote corners of the tropics.

(Though not too remote for profit to find.)

Enter the Star of the Forest,
Didymoplexis stella-silvae.
One of sixteen new orchids found
from a once dense corner of Madagascar.

No leaves or chlorophyll,
a plant that has lost what makes a plant.
Star-like flowers that arise out of the dank humus
for one day of attraction

in the total darkness.

The pollinator a mystery, though ants
are suspected.
The lucky one.

3 of the 16 orchids are already extinct
due to logging and geranium oil
for aromatherapy in sweet smelling
middle-class Western homes.

The Whirlpool

Held in the vertex of two fixed points
a marriage finger-long whirlpool spins
on an axis made of flux and micro
-currents cut and bled by stony grins.
Constantly changing, tugged by tides
that tear galaxies from rotating points.
Shrinking and growing, a tiny black
hole of indecision that suddenly hides,
consuming itself, now spooling anew
or two passing twigs sharing a cause,
locked in a dance of undulating spirals
as if the river was crafting metaphors
of how life works, how my soul clings
to a spinning body of water and wind.

Rabbit, Being

You seem unafraid
of my borrowing

just briefly
the being of you

alphabeting the path ahead.
Lolloping timeless child

veering into the grass,
unhurried chewing,

the sun of California
poppies in your ears.

I twitch past, taking
back my form,

and you flow
into the entanglement

of undergrowth
and words.

The Song of Night

Riding past a pond near the Deschutes River
a song uncoils up from the ink of creation,
something hidden and unheard until now:
frog song, fat with hope and moist heart.
Thousands of thirsting, unafraid frogs
quivering with darkening desire. I think
of all the still trees at night, trillions of trees
packed darkly with billions of huddled birds
keeping deathly quiet and so still you forget
they even exist until the sun summons them
and orders the moths to become indifference.
Even in the alley outside, the frogs sing June,
writing themselves alive out of concrete,
cats, cars and the fading of the music sheet.

The Vastness

When the first star appears
in the chalking evening night
between the almost finished green silhouettes
of two divine Douglas firs

I know poetry.

So does the dog,
huffing with the fever of fetch,
an enthusiasm to make gods proud.

Two bats swirl around dark statements of tree,
bouncing between belief and myth.

Hairs on my leg tingle with needling
explorers with as much right to needing
as the dog who noses
the vastness of the grass,
trying to find his joy.

On Hearing 'River Snow' by Liu Zongyuan Recited in Chinese

Grade 4 faces look up at me. International school in China.
Too many poems to choose from. All human traces.
On Zoom, collar shirt, beard, middle aged man.
Not alone. Dangling poems in the keen river. Smiles.

Then the Chinese teacher starts a recital of the 'River Snow' by Liu Zongyuan, to rudder the students' recall of shared knowledge. Instantly, they serenade in Chinese. For a few seconds I am with the river snow, the climbable mountain, knowledge we are not alone.

Deschutes' Circles

An osprey curves up to its nest,
fish fixed in a flapping grimace.
Chicks cry out with oval hunger.

At the river bandstand older adults
sit in a fenced-off 'O' discussing April's
aches around an open box of donuts.

On the picnic lawn Canada geese bob
heads and hiss to warn the walkers
away from the easter-yellow gifts.

On the arching Old Mill footbridge
flags the color of an invaded nation
flap and flank in a violent wind.

The river's wisdom bends, breaks it-
self around rocks, mends with curling
currents and the ocean's distant O.

Ukiyo-e in Oregon

The Canada geese know Hiroshige's
signal: that shock of first snow
that pastes the Cascades. They wheel

around the Deschutes River, practicing
floating formations, feeling the wind
for the resistance to leave, cleave

into V's of grief. The first formation
line up uneven necklace over the strung
outline of the peaks, perfectly composed.

The next day, ducks stir up in chaotic
copying. A rare morning full moon
hangs between Bachelor and Broken Top.

Its stained pearl eye winks at Vincent
and sinks into the gulping Pacific, permission
for all to leave and arrive elsewhere.

Skunk Dying

I stop by a cabal
of walkers, push-carts and beards
oracling the origin of

a black lump shivering on the side
of the Mosier Twin Tunnels
trail.
A skunk
with its tail

curled around and slapped flat.

A devotee approaches, offering
water on tinfoil.

Hit by a bike—the agreement.

Then the devotees turn and leave
without witnessing resurrection.

When I run back, the skunk
is closed up, trembling,
tinfoil its death totem.

I have nothing to offer.
Everything is left to waste.

The Horned Owl Gathers

Some blessed Hope, whereof he knew
And I was unaware.
—Thomas Hardy

We hear the pair beckoning an audience
from a ponderosa pine pinned between
toffee-colored cliffs and the syrupy river.
My wife first sees the storybook silhouette
owl: ear tufts, turning head, a wink of wings.
We watch him call and bob, mate replying
higher up, hidden by the foliage discretion.

Two runners stop, drawn by our homage.
We tell them there's owls up there, a gift
heard in passing but rarely seen given.
Now there is a small band of us, watching
the performance, deserving our applause.
Post-pandemic loners share pellets of news,
our humanity, the sharing of hidden views.

Hummingbird Versus Cat

Beloved Cat
a child in the eyes of its owner

stalks Hummingbird
and makes shocking leap, swatting

the air milliseconds away from fatality.
Hummingbird swivels on its pointed heels

and looks down at the Orange Devil
and zealot of the Domestic Jaguar God,

representative of so much songbird silence.
With a prayer to Huitzilopochtli, she

stabs forward twice, tiny goading
god of war, lord of gold, the sun itself,

able to see colors that gasp rainbows.
Then zips up exhausted into the tree, far

from the befuddled fur below
looking up at a sky

Hummingbird saved back in the days
when jaguar feared feathers.

Song for Decaying Angler Fish

Far from the lip of the low tide line
lays the flattened oval dome of a head
set in a sulking death grimace. A thin
line of a spine tailed out behind, past
two flailing flags that were once fins.
Here Be a Monster from Beyond
the Twilight Zone, a taunter of tiny
morsels lured by the angling light.
What roll and pitch of fate brought
this fat mouth of life and death up
from the depths to find its bleaching
peace on the beach of Pacific City?
Children scream, the waves roll on.
Even decay has its own sweet song.

The Gray Whale

A couple on the Pelican Brewery veranda
point it out. A spouting jet of breath to the left

of the kite-surfer. Another couple join
in the watch and we all call out in surprise

when the sea breaks and the dark frown
of the breaching body follows the familiar jet

(that I later learn from Ellen can appear close-
up like a heart thanks to two blowholes.)

Humpback whale, insists the man in a neon
yellow cagoule on a heatwave week. I don't

correct him—save it for the polite distance
of a poem. Oregon coast gray whale,

the greatest of all migrators, save for a few
residents taking advantage of easy dining,

gifted now like how my parents gave me
a small present on my brother's birthday

(and vice-versa). I follow the vague line of
hope south as the gray whale marks

a rare return to Nestucca bay. Three times,
I share but by the end the couples had gone

back to quiet conversations and screens.
There came a time in my childhood

when my parents told me I was old enough
to know I didn’t need a consolation gift

in place for emotional understanding.
Being the oldest, I was first to lose.

But I still don’t feel old enough to receive,
and I will keep looking for that whale.

Whale Blessing

Coffees in hand we scan coastal waters where immigrants are cruising from California calving to the colder waters north, hoping to find sustenance in the emptying waters. A gushing spray miles out causes fuss. Binoculars out we hunt, following the white wheel of birds monitoring bubbles. The privilege of a panoramic window in a rented house on the Bandon coast; expectations of Nature demanded by the gaping glass. There is talk of a breech. Too hard to see definitively, we combat the puff of disappointment too shallow to be named. We owe the whales an opaque passage after centuries of greasing the carnivorous light of human progress. Creatures of song and grief reduced to corsets and lamps. About to give up, a bald eagle passes by the window, reminding us to look closer to home and stop scavenging for gifts that are no longer ours to take.

The Owl

Owl sings

a shock

that shakes
you off the phone, WIFI worry.

Yes, there is still Nature out there.
Something alien
to your remotely controlled world.

It is an ancient world
indifferent to your aches,

The call is a shriek from what
you found as a child

and lost. The contraction
of a sylvan heart.

Redemption is being offered.

Let Athena's messenger in.

Remember.

After the Open-Mic Reading

tree swallows electrify the river
as the waxing gibbous moon plays
nucleus to the evening's sighing cell.

Charged with hunger, the swallows clot
in giddy spots, swaying like a hundred
beckoning Thai-Chi hands, both bodies
and waves of energy at once. I am in awe

of the readers who stand at open mics:
gaping souls, fluxing identities, pain
screamed so softly they become
swallows without the wings.

For All the Alligators

I

They rolled their eyes
and clenched their jaws when I told them.

Just look out of the window, they're everywhere. Pests.

But we don't have alligators in Oregon,
or even England where I crawled from.
Theme parks take the awe out of discovery,
the thirst to find and be found.

II

Most Uber drivers wouldn't go to Lake Tohopekaliga,
afraid to be eaten by rush hour traffic.
Adronik from Venezuela was different.
Maracaibo, he insisted. Not Caracas. Bad place.
He snaked through the hungry traffic, apologizing
for his English but glad to be talking.
Everyone in Florida speaks Spanish!

III

The world of highways and apps ends.
Now the place for post-poised hawks,
stalking herons, posing white egrets,
and our airboat skimming reeds and lily pads
floating across make-believe water
as if it knew this life is just one long dream.

We saw them right away, creeping into the night,
suspicious eyeballs and snouts, slithering s's of swimming tails,
a child washing a paint brush.

The boat was full of fellow Brits with questions,
quips. A Welsh mother praised the beauty
of the sunset leaking on the lake surface,
the upturned pail of the storm dumping the horizon.

Our captain earned his tips by finding
a giant male who sat unmoved by our compliments.
For ten minutes he ate any idea of Orlando,
Disneyfied nature and inflated costs. Only
the roar of the fan engine annoyed him enough.

No tips from the Brits. Their dollars stayed
firmly hidden under cultural waters.

IV

I stayed for the evening tour and the captain's
same jokes: only captained twice, the gators eat
ex-wives and mother-in-laws. Sexism
not an issue here. A mother from Ohio
mock-snapped at her teenage son for
talking of the Hood never leaving her.
Homework help? Not me. Ask Google.
He just wants $300 designer sneakers.
Throw the children in, the captain advised.

The dark lake was smothered with night flies
and the flash of the captain's torch, searching
for the fire reflection in the monsters' eyes.
All wading birds became prehistoric statues.
The smaller gators were out—sneaky bodies,
sudden eyes, darting under water when we roared

too close. I grieved to leave the lake, the deathly
quiet world of heron, lily and storm-lit skies,
the old masters of the undecided order, above
and below, all the more beautiful for being both.

V

The taxi took me back to the world of highways lined
with movie-dark motels, signs for pizza, massages,
Disney toy discounts, billboards boasting so many
supposedly won legal battles. I felt eaten alive by neon
and in more danger than eye-to-eye with giants.

What Children Already Know

They say heavy snow is coming tomorrow.

Today, the sky is an upturned ocean.
A boat scars it, heading east.

The pine trees rock gently
while they can, every needle
trembling in time.

My Hong Kong lucky cat paws the air
as if sensing the mousey fortune.

I aim to be like the children
rushing to the classroom window,

gasping at the sudden suffocating
of the world they think they know,

the metamorphosis the ancient Greeks
built myths around. Only now,

in my middle years
with my lesson suspended

and the window crowded by wowing,
am I ready to change, re-learn

what children already know.

The Song of a Pink Dogwood Tree

As if knowing that the wooden blue block
rising out of a churned-up garden, ringed
by stumps of once star-straining pines,
fussed over by workers cursing in tongues
is a Babel offering to carving profit
out of the tiniest plots (with river views),
the pink dogwood tree excels itself with
thousands of pink stars fed by supernovae
saved in the wise roots since last summer.
The effort to fill every fractal fission is far
more fruitful than the tower we christen
'The Portaloo,' more spectacular than stars.
Block and tree are owned by the neighbor.
I know which prophet is worth the labor.

The Salmon Bake

Walking to the university we watch
a raven battle a bald eagle,
trying to drive it out of its sky.

In the worried line for the Salmon Bake
and Traditional Side Dishes
we're informed: no more salmon.

So sorry. It's run out, all of it.
Yes, we know you pre-booked tickets.
We didn't expect so many

White Guardians piling up plates.
If only they'd dammed them
rather than Celilo Falls. White Greed

up front defeats White Hope behind.
The Chancellor promises refunds,
even to those who emptied the river.

Existing profits will cover human error,
computer system—old and new
excuses. We scrape a meal from bones

and smiles from sorrowful Reservation
staff. The menu another betrayed treaty.
Still, the Drumming Circle will play.

The indigenous band won a Grammy.
Now they charge thousands an hour.
The refund takes weeks to come.

In Yellowjacket Heaven

there are gigantic bags
full of sticky treats
and the writhing bodies
of human homeowners,
the screams of mercy
drowned out by the buzz
of wasps wondering
what good are human
swarms that ignore
seasons, suck the sap
out of every flower,
act as if the miracle
of being was only theirs
to keep out of the bag.

Flying Kites at Namche Bazaar, Nepal

On a stony, bare palm of land
held aloft a bent wrist of a valley

children as small as Harry Lime's
ants flew kites, tiny red and blue

birds that blessed the terraced town
with a memory more moving

than the surrounding mountains,
geisha-ed in cloud and snow.

Namche Bazaar. That name spell-
ing pounding heart, supplying

the base camp of my belief
that the smallest steps matter.

The Snow Tornado

I want to show you
what swirled into being
in between the creamy,
cracked cliffs topped
with confident office
blocks that will one day
decay due to erosion,
and the duck-dotted,
ice-veined river
that will one day
dry up due to us.
Just a few seconds
for the white genie
in a slushy desert
to pirouette
circles and
then gasp
itself
out
of

III.
ARTIFICIALIA

In My Life

My neighbors have wind chimes
that drown out
the impatience of Highway 97

and sometimes passing birds.

It plays the first two notes of 'In My Life'
over and over
again
wanting me
to be wistful about homes

I have left and lost and found.

Autumn, it stopped.

A young woman sat in the backyard,
singing love ballads at the top of her voice,
disturbing birds, social plans
and then suddenly crying

siren, always sirens on 97.

Winter and the tears stop.

The wind chime is back
with its lyrics of home.

Looking Down

Looking up in wonder I see
the bald eagle staring down,

circling over the bridge
like a confused current.

What can she make of the river,
that old logging lane, clogged

by floaters, drinks in hand
toasting the neon dying sky

(smokey sunsets make the best photographs)

the raggedly rising
"affordable" accommodation

(mountain views the premium)

the outskirts of her territory
dotted with damp, illegal tents

(deaths every winter, no laws change)

the zip and buzz of teenagers
on ebikes, flirting with bare-headed fate

(laws will change once the deaths increase)

the countless California plates
that so frustrates the truck drivers

(isn’t everyone an immigrant somewhere?)

the empty recall of fly-fishers
and a river spitting out fewer swallows, flies

(hooks too large to catch microplastics) . . .

The bald eagle turns away,
gifting itself to the sigh-blue sky.

An Osprey and a Traffic Circle

An osprey rises on its hungry hopes and

hovers,
cutlass wings preparing for purpose.

She works her way down the tendon
of the river as the road clogs with the cholesterol of the homeward bound.

She conducts her hunting symphony
as cars heap into the traffic circle, honking,

observed by three still rock chucks, twitching white noses,
resurrected recently from winter

to find their view smaller than last year.

Osprey disappears. Rock chucks duck for cover.
The road remains close to rupture.

A Bottle Longs to Be Reunited with Its Owner

after Aliyah Cotton

You call me convenient,
snatching me off a shelf
for a brief exchange of fluids.
You gulp me, and I taste
your rush to use me up.

I gift you miniscule parts
of my fracturing self.

Then you toss me aside like a regrettable date.

I am patient. For hundreds
of years, I will lay waiting for you.

You might find me floating,
a Man (made) of War, trashy tentacles
curling in currents of inaction.

Sometimes I sink and settle
on a heap of other lonely loungers.

There I break down
flaking in the water, into finer and finer particles,
gulped down, embedding in your sea-meat,
or filtering through the air, falling
back down to you as plastic rain.

Eventually,
you'll drink me again,

and I'll coalesce in hidden currents
of your body,
never to leave,
so we can finally become one.

A Traffic Circle in Bend, OR

Three deer clatter the early morning road,
racing to the traffic circle.
They mount
the mound and look around.

The lead doe stands

on the hump with the abstract art, ears
pinned back, alert while the others slip
into the moat to eat, bovine brains awash
with hunger, pheromones,
the loss of
woods.

Further down road there's another traffic circle
crowned with metal deer.
                                        Metal salmon
are remembered in another circle.

When the Deschutes River runs so low
the floating tourists scrape their rubber rings
and beer can cling on the rocks,
water murals will splash
the million-dollar homes,
and glacial reliefs will flow
across all the new walls,
and someone will commission raindrops
to remind us of tears.

Getting Gas in Roseburg, OR

Car bleeping empty, we roll into the gas station
on a disinterested strip in Roseburg.

A woman picks up the pump, arms just as thin,
skin crinkled by too many stories.

We exchange pleasantries about the town,
wondering what can make her smile

through such cracked teeth. She talks
Chicago suburbs, sirens and gunshots.

None of that around here, just happy people,
thank Jesus for it all. She thanks Jesus

a few more times, finishing refueling
faith. Why not God in the gas pump?

His creatures small propelling His creatures great.
The consequences of freewill do not hesitate.

Wisdom Versus Experience

At a patio table of an expensive lodge
overlooking the High Cascades with little
lingering snow, four friends in their elder

days talk about a fifth friend who worked
too hard, giving his all and died before
he could enjoy the views he longed for,

about that holiday rental in Mexico,
vast bedrooms overlooking an ocean
'two little women' doing all the cooking,

the beers, sports, home improvements,
an irritating mutual friend, grandchildren.
the pitter and patter of aging friendship.

All the while the wildfire threat was 'high,'
the glaciers becoming indigenous myths.

Skeleton Doll

At Riley Ranch parents watch as
their girls clamber a fallen fir tree.
The onesie-wrapped one wanders
near the enchanted roots, amused
by the woody writhing and rhythm
of slow death. Her staircase into
the hidden is lined with English
and Spanish words of warning.
Be careful. N*o tan lejos.* In her hands
a skeleton doll rocks plastic joints,
a month before *Día de los Muertos.*
Sudden crash and tearing tears.
Parental voices guide her back.
The doll is first out of the crack.

The Grapes

Standing in Safeway staring
at grapes, a man approaches.
I heard him talk to his sons

with a soft, operatic Spanish.
Inspired by our indecision
he teaches us about the fruit

which ones are sweet and soft,
the ones that crunch—his son's
favorites. He is from Chile,

works in agriculture—grapes,
green and red. Those ones.
Recommends with a smile.

Later we eat grapes and thank
life for the small, sweet gifts.

Small World, Skyler

My wife apologizing for her excitement
seeing the secretary of a school she worked at 13 years ago.

Small world.
For Skyler—

who pumps the gas in the Madras Safeway—
there is no Thanksgiving gathering.

He's young, he says. Works holidays. For the money.

My wife says our car is loaded like we're moving,
but it's just a few days with family.

His car is always loaded with cables, batteries, tools.
He's saved 25 people around here.

Likes to fix cars, open them up. Surgery.
But not hybrids. Too much electronics.

He likes to keep the world uncomplicated, local.
We drive off, tank full, strangely sad.

The Pack

Middle School boys meander,
a collective of tanned, lengthening legs,
Hawaiian shorts, the latest white crocs.

They skirt the Box Factory.
Decades before they were born,
boxes were sliced out of lumber.
Now it's grown-up breweries, bars,
specialized exercise, Modern Games.

The tallest boy with the deepest voice
barks at a cider bar, then steals
a dog bone shaped treat from
a table outside a closed winery.
He dares his mutts to eat one.
The runt of the pack grabs it,
makes to gobble it down.
"Not even that bad!"

"You ate it?"

"No, but I could!" he howls,

and the pack laughs.
He retreats to the back
to lick his wounds.

The pack pile into the supermarket
priced higher for local homeowners
and thrift through $5 notes,
asking how much everything costs,
taking pictures on phones, dares, dares.

Transient Moon

They say nothing new can be said
about the moon. So instead I'll let
it set over the white shy Cascades,
the carpark of the economy hotel,
license plates from across the country,
even Alaska and Hawaii. Some cars
are marred, bulging with a life scarred
by changing plans. Cigarette smoke
loiters in the land left undeveloped.
Weary bodies huddled in hesitations.
Unleashed dogs snag at the bushes.
This poem's moon does not guard
these people. Medieval in needs,
they look to the road to be freed.

Three First-Grade Boys on the Titanic

Three boys squat
in the Book Corner
looking down
at the open heart of history.

One boy exclaims:
I wish I was on the Titanic.

Another replies with logic:
You can't be on it.

A third who knows about attention
and the need to make an impact
to be noticed, to exist, states:
I was on the Titanic. I was, I was!

The two other boys don't respond,
just keeping looking down at the picture
of the ship being sundered, closing
around the book like a prayer,

while the third, silently ousted,
wonders if his lie was in fact a kind of truth.

A Steiner Piano Shop

There's a Steiner Piano Shop in Lake Oswego now.
The millionaires who wow the lake in record numbers,

in palaces policed by cameras, scraped and landscaped
by immigrant workers, stocked with pouty power boats

and gleaming Teslas can now insist their children clatter
through Mozart whilst they plan weekend wake-surfing

on the lake, too dirty to swim in, and family trips
to the Caribbean, second homes, thanking God

there's no homeless camps and fentanyl addiction
in their downtown. Close the gate, security cameras on,

kids all tucked up with the latest fairy tale mirrors
while the dog roams its empty, echoing territory.

Long Way

In the carpark of My Place Hotel
where battered cars crammed with
life's fractured essentials collect, two
railroad repair men stand stoking

a small portable barbeque, looking
around for Fire Department dudes
who yesterday told them to quench
their open fire that saved them buying

4th July \$30 burgers from Doordash.
Sophie, our friends' Frenchie, sniffs
out their story. The girder-slim older man
with a late summer sagebrush beard

does the talking. *We put fires out*
for a living. All across the States. No risks.
The younger, broader man pets Sophie,
tickles himself into smiles and nods.

Oregon—long way from home. Oklahoma.
Go back that way soon. Sophie could stay
forever, but an old body needs its couch.
In six months, she will be suddenly dead,

and my wife and I grieving all over again,
the two railroad men fixing up East,
the My Place Hotel deck reshuffled,
and fires, fires, fires everywhere.

Prayer for a Certain Type of Truck Driver

In my less spiritual moments when I am riding my bike in my hometown or on narrow coastal roads, I pray that a certain type of truck driver—alternative American flags flying, slogans blaring swear words about presidents, engines revving full penile throttle, the farts of toxic black smoke, windows winding down so a wish-I-was-a-wanna-be quarterback can shout at me to get off my expletive bike or raise a finger—suddenly breaks down in the middle of their nowhere, engine sputtering, no idea why, just a molten manhood. Maybe they find redemption in the realization that a bike might not be so bad after all. Or that poetry can make a difference. But I doubt it.

Free Refills

My American family like to retell the story
of the first time in a West Coast restaurant

when a waitress offered more lemonade.
I hesitated, not wanting to spend too much.

But everyone chorused: free refills, free refills.
Disbelief crossed my working-class British face.

Yes, free.

My dad's mantra: only things free in life
are taxes, the weather and death.

So I drank three pints as if the world was ending
and marveled in dreams and bladders.

Cleaning Caravans

To have a foreign holiday, progress.
Their parents never left England.
Retirement savings not enough.
Every Saturday they labored, cleaning

the caravans in Goodrington Park.
Grandad did hoovering and dusting,
Nan the heavy lifting: the stove, sinks,
kitchens. No one spoke of bathrooms.

Two hours tops before the next punters.
The whole summer season to save up
for two months in Benidorm, Spain.
All the caravan cleaning money spent

for foreign sunshine in the cold winter.
Granddad shared the swimming pool
with old war enemies, no one speaking,
rivalry resurrected over towel placement.

They returned to spring and a pension.
Same summer work, never spoken about.
Shame and pride mixed with sangria—
a particularly working-class cocktail.

Over the years, the prices crept up,
cleaning caravans lost their sparkle.
Keys handed in. One final trip. A toast
to hard work, the sea, old enemies.

Beyond the Mail

Stars, hide your fires;
Let not light see my black and deep desires.
—Macbeth

At a UPS postal store explaining
to a High School Saturday worker
that I want postcards to go to nephews
and friends in England and Switzerland.

Questions call over her supervisor, a
young man with an unwashed ponytail.
Sniffing error and a chance to teach,
he makes corrections, directs the girl

how to weigh and till the mail, special
stamps needed, which buttons to press.
All the while she's looking up at me,
eyes widening in the exasperation of

teenage girls being directed by the full-
time Dude: part-priest, part-wishful
thinking. He professes heart-heated
assertions that he makes the same mistakes,

that having the stamp paper stick out
like a lip means less chance of clogging—
it happens, not often, but he wants
to show her the right way to do things,

useful skills for life beyond the mail.
He fists down the stamps with weighty
force, compensating for pencil arms,
the small chances of being read by her.

The Springs

Ernie the mattress salesman king
of an empty empire greets us
open arms, cratered face,
a half-life how can I help you folks?

We explain needs, inquire about charges,
dreading the hard sale,
and he warms up a little, inviting
us to try his spring mattress versus memory
foam. Gives us his honest opinion:
springs for him, always springs.

Ready to leave, my wife says *ciao.*
Something returns in Ernie's eyes.
Been years since I heard that.

It takes little prodding for him to confess
seven years in Italy after the military:
Italian wife, (*bella, bella*), living in Forte dei Marmi,
(*Papa knew marble like the back of his hand*),
skiing up in the alps, old men playing
pianoforte in Medieval towers,
spring time, the cafés, appetizers,
the wine (*ah, the wine*) . . .

He bounced from memory to memory,
a child trampolining on a bed,
a younger man foaming the cappuccino.

We felt pain to leave him,
a Cheshire Cat, sinking back
into the shifting sleepiness of later life.

Dear Life

I can’t give them up,
Dad tells me. More confessions:
I’ve never read them either.

Books he bought as a teenager:
omnibus editions from Pullingers,
the first object he could own.

Childhood spent in a home loaned
from a landlord, from the street’s
pebbled playground, from the land—
vegetable plots and chickens
pecking around the Anderson shelter.

He built a shelf in his bedroom
to honor his first books, relics
for a shrine of a world to come.

Now, 76, he admits
he does not want to stop renting.
He is hanging onto them
for dear life.

Half

He jutted out of the ebike shop
and spluttered about my shoes.

I misunderstood his ungluing
words from the sticky half of his brain.

We made small talk as he ached
his right leg forward, biting breath,

a rupture of unnecessary apologies,
half smiles from a head half bald

and half overgrown. Did no one cut it?
He told me his right side doesn't work

in a sentence as long as guilt and pity.

That's his bike, the yellow one.
He wants it to go all-terrain.
Waiting for the parts to come from—

points up—

tries to name the city in a slur.

I guess: Portland, Seattle, Vancouver,
I overshot with Anchorage.
Acha-Cagaga
Canada!
We both punch the air.

My wife finds us like old friends.

We wish him safe travels.
in all senses insufficient.

TikTok Lockdown

A letter was left in the bathroom.
A promise of a shooting
threatened in all high schools—on TikTok.

*

Whole school scared into lockdown.

5 hours.

Armed police in corridors,
Escorts to the bathroom.

*

In her Physics class
the teacher tries a lesson:
The Physics of Shooting.

Students end up playing card games,
lectures on swearing.

*

The following day
—The promised Day of Death—
is a non-academic choice day.

Most start the holidays early.

*

Post-holidays and one teacher
bought a toilet-bucket for the classroom.

No joke, she assures me.
It has a privacy curtain. Check it out:

Amazon.com: Camco 41549 Portable 5-Gallon Toilet Bucket with Seat and Lid Attachment | Lightweight and Easy to Clean | Great for Camping, Hiking, Hunting and More , Blue : Automotive

For those really long sessions
and not wanting to be escorted by armed police

or if the police don't come

in time.

Between

I

Between High 97 and cement trucks
on a paved path to a brewery
the wreckage of a life spills over:

unwashed clothes, decomposing bags,
a tattered shelter torn up by the tornado
of sudden misfortunes, all piling up.

In the heart of it all, a hooded man
rubbing his hands, foraging.

We approached, tensing the dog's leash.

The castaway looks up.
A cleanly shaken middle aged realtor face.
"Sorry, just tidying up my house."

We tell him, no problem.

"God bless you, have a nice night."

We stumble on, marveling
at our own misconceptions.

II

In the barbers the buzz-talk is of the homeless
as meth-head vermin who thin out, grow back,
shank you—pond scum, one customer says.
The room is full of reminiscences about Old Bend
and the one homeless man: a quirky character
who would walk around town talking to himself.
Harmless. A touch of color in the lumber town.
Not this plague of non-people who die non-deaths
in the winter and heat-stroked, wildfired summers.

III

My niece teaches me with the wisdom of the young about
Aggressive Architecture: bus shelter benches too short to sleep on,
and park benches with armrests, scree of stones spilt on tempting
tent land. I had always wondered why. She tells me I can't unsee
them now, and she's right.

Haiku

Teenager passing
Your dog looks like a fat pig!
Dog keeps pissing.

Reflecting off snow
city lights fill the darkness—
good night stars

Birthday surprise—
snowflakes sparkling
in the June sun.

No cars stop for the
homeless man at the crosswalk . . .
coffee tastes better.

April brings hope.
Elderly care-home old man
refills bird feeder.

In pouring rain
immigrant sells flowers—
Americans dream

Flat tires, feet spasm,
clothes spilling from car door—
Americans dream

IV.
SCIENTIFICA

The Poet, God

In the beginning,
God wrote infinitely before a spaceless window
open to the void.

Perhaps disliking the work, God threw
all the poems out of the window
and they coalesced and swirled and erupted
into the universe, forming
atoms and the Chapbook of Elements,
then the Epic of the DNA,
The Collected Poems of Life
with award-winning variety, words in all forms,
and finally us, with our elevated word-souls,
reconstructing all that fractured work
in our little imitations of infinity
and offering it back up to God
as prayer or questions or proof.

God does not respond, does not read
the overwhelming volume of submissions.
God has angelic interns to do that.

God sits procrastinating over a new volume,
trying always to write the perfect poem,
aware, like all poets,
that no such poem exists
and the closest you can come to it
is being it.

Ode to Joy

In the morning, I find young maples
clinging to the sheer face of the cliff
on the Mosier Tunnels trail. Naked
roots on the black wet wall, no soil.

In the evening, we take dinner to Joy,
alone now her husband's suffering
has ended. Dwarfed by darkness, she
finds strength telling any story of him.

Few tears today, the first time. I wish
we had met when laughter was a water-
fall, not a diverted river of grief. She
recounts memories mixed with quick

sickness, the sudden need for family
to gather: build ramps, decking access
with a view of an inoperable volcano.
Words like 'sarcoma' and 'lung spots'

stick as she picks at the roast chicken.
A stroke after a COVID vaccine. Doubt
lingers in an unfinished mouthful. Still
she laughs, grateful for dinner, company.

Complementing our marriage reminds
hers of 51 years. She talks in present tense.
He's still here. Below, the Columbia River
continues carving, the volcano sleeping.

The Box

Mid July limps under a heatwave,
the hottest records in the Pacific Northwest.

This will not be the last
now the box is open.

The sticky tarmac heaves with huge pandora moths,
slapping their wings, refusing to submit
to the current in their life cycle,
an outbreak of overlapping generations
that occurs every few decades.

Did these adults get a chance to lay
futures in the high desert pine trees
before they fell from a place of illusion,
or were they exposed to a future
they cannot adapt to

now the box is open?

The Under

It begins with a kestrel.

The boys and I watch it well up
and hold the Alpine valley
under hyperactive wings.

It's beak and eye focus us on the
under,

the small zone of springing surprises:
a flower suddenly found,
a bee jabbing us back,
springing crickets and baby grasshoppers.

For an age, the boys and I wrestle
the jungle with the Biblical order
of our giant, distributive feet.

Now the Enlightenment: classifying,
quantifying, identifying in all the ways
children point, question, gasp,
want to know more, find more.

I teach the boys to catch crickets
with Newtonian cause and effect.
We release them with Eastern kindness
so they can return to the under

and the eyeing wings above.

The Rose

It wasn't the years my parents spent growing roses, battling aphids, cultivating color in our front garden, the jagged thorns making their point.

It wasn't reading Rilke's poems, seeing his grave in Raron, the inscription talking about the divinity that unfolds in the petals, the depth of his poems.

It was a small rose bush my wife bought for our concrete backyard garden: a landing strip of scattered soil and bark chips just wide enough for the pot.

It was the very first yellow flower that proved the bud's potential unfolding into a spiraling galaxy of yellow, bigger than the original expansion.

It was my wife's joy in the art of cultivation, in the handling of love that could not be given to the intended but could be sown and seen nonetheless.

Cape Kiwanda

In Café Stimulus we watch
the impetus of white hands
closing above Cape Kiwanda.

A few seconds of bursting fists,
then a claw brought scraping
down the Cape's extended leg

of land, a brief white waterfall
weeping into the wet rock,
the base thump of the sea,

pulse of the inevitable tsunami
promised in evacuation maps,
pointing safety that way, away

from dune-heaped holiday
homes no one's really ready
to flee from. One shuddering

day the shaken sea will rise
and a Great Hand will wave
us away, white water weeping

into wet, indifferent rock.
Until then, we buy and sell,
surf the swell, drink coffee.

Unenforceable

In the carpark of the McPhillips Beach State Park
a ranger opens up a black hole
and approaches the galaxy of indulgence.

Despite all the warning signs in the park,
the beach, in town,
fireworks
are still bought and blown up
to rattle the air in celebration of a war
won hundreds of years ago,
most facts forgotten by those who cheer,
beers in hands, no thought to what comes
down
to worsen our wildfire washed air.

"We tried enforcing but they fired
them at us. Even at the Sheriff.
So what can you do?" Shrugs and

begins snapping at the spew of trash,
hoping his bag's gravity is enough.

Calculating the Cost

I want to say to the student stressing
about the next math test, worrying her
score will never reflect her best, the
trauma adding up, she fears the rest,
that stupid tests are not the real math.
It's just the system of keeping account,
creating a product that can have skill
enough to add up spending amounts.
Math is a bee's hexagon honeycomb,
the minutes since you last saw your love
the distance the sun hopes to roam,
the fractal divisions of the trees above,
the sum of all our warming actions,
the urgent need of healing subtractions.

Elegy for the Caught Fish

I

Over the Salem highway flies
A bald eagle carrying a fish like a weed out of the Willamette.
We totem our empires with the raptor,
weave into flags, fix on coins
but what of the victims?
How come no one ever glories the fish

for fighting its way from the ocean
and then giving itself up
so that eagle chicks can grow?
We are all too busy dreaming the eagle,
afraid to admit that in life
we are more often the fish.

II

At Suttle Lake two osprey hang on winds,
suspended W's questioning the timing
of the sockeye's surge from the Pacific
via the Columbia, Metolius, Suttle Creek.
A bald eagle joins in the salivating search,
the white tail of false truce flying.

I wish them all failure for I am now
with the fish, that fighter, finder of fortune
in the gravel and grains of shallow water.
All that effort deserves more than death
in sudden claws before being spawn-weary
and purpose-filled, empty of any need.

Hope in January

after Emily Dickinson

Hope is also today in January:
a held breathe of a day, sky
fluttered with a few feathers,
lingering leaves, everything
agreeing that this lovely lie
is—Really—worth believing.

The Wisdom of Photons

I believe a leaf of grass is no less
than the journey-work of the stars
—Walt Whitman

I wake up in the middle of the night.
A single star winks at me. Photons fired
out thousands, maybe millions of years ago,
skimming space, slipping solar systems,
sneaking past planets—one true beam
sometimes bent by the gulp of gravity,

but always adhering to its lucky destination.
Looking at starlight, I feel the glaring truth:
on the long road of Order to Disorder—
a journey of trillions of years uncountable
in this fleeting human mind—I am just
a flicker, a tiny finger of light and heat,

hardly noticeable in this minuscule moment,
yet a flame nonetheless, with heat and light
and worth and rage. So I must try to shine,
shine all the brighter for the dying light I am.
I thank the photons for teaching me. What
they lack in mass they make up for in wisdom.

Of Love and Atoms

Let us think of love
not as a miracle of chance

meetings, carefully chosen
words, promises and pain, heart

beats and bursts of hormones,
buds of May, never part darlings,

but instead a ridiculously unlikely
event gifted by bonded atoms

made mostly out of empty space,
so little matter that it is a wonder

that we can even hold hands,
that we are only giddy ghosts

that kiss through each other
on the short chase to infinity.

Different River

On the bank of the Deschutes River,
past the dog turds,
out of the way of the walkers
talking loudly in passing barks,

the river is wide, shallow, slashed
with boulders that tear the silk ragged.
Panic attacks on halt.

Here I meditate in March,
the warming afternoon sun kaleidoscoping
closed eyelids, iPhone app counting
down the ten minutes of me-time.

When I open my eyes,
a different river before me.

Journeying geese rally against the tide,
the whistle of duck wings,
gusts of wind turn the water's top
so that new waves steal the sunlight's jewels,
spills and sinks them sparkling.

Darker, slower, older. It takes me time
to adjust and wander off home,
changed, Heraclitus rolling his eyes.

This Earth Day

I happen to look
up into a ponderosa pine,
attracted by a squeaking energy.

A pair of pygmy nuthatches,
no bigger than my thumb
play out a private parlor game:

she with gifted white fluff in her bill,
he vibrating his tiny wings,
dancing as if the entire world

was just this potential mate,
the branch that holds her,
the eggs they might make.

I dare not move on, knowing
how soon it will all be gone.

Objection

While we stretch on mats one mom
sighs about a client who objected
to her daughter dancing in a hood.
Too much like a witch. Take it off!

Falsely accused because of a belief
in a Taylor Swift inspired hoodie.
This ignites our instructor to confess
a scolded family history: 17th century

ancestor midwife-wise woman
convicted of being a witch, exiled
from Boston, two daughters burned
at the stake, fanned by male fear.

Maybe Taylor could write a song
about objections that are never wrong.

Mother-in-Law Versus Fate

We return to her sitting on the bench
headphones on, waving at us, all smiles.
She tells us about the black bear she saw
clambering along a nearby log. Walkers
pointed it out and then rushed on. She sat
and watched, unafraid. Can't run anymore.
Phone? Who knows where? Bear huffed
back into the shadows, soon to be gone.
We drive into Hood River valley awash
with a sea-spill of new pear tree blossom,
Waves of quite wonderful white while
in the background mournful Mount Hood
sings last winter's snow and ice songs,
shrinking chords of time soon to be gone.

Running Across Oregon

We meet at White Water Falls where water
from Mount Hood comes drumming down
after a double marathon tumble. His torrent
of unkempt hair damned by a bandana badly
in need of a wash. He talks like a doped-up
time-traveler from the Summer of Love,
apologizing for leaving his car door open
and making us wait. 'Running Across Oregon'
chalked on the rear window. His brother
is with him and pregnant wife, seven months.
Spending as much time together as they can,
running south to north, they camp anywhere,
sleep in the car. Twenty-seven, already knows:
Oregon is the best, but so many miles to go.

Sunflower

Stamen stand to attention, parading
rippling hearts and radiating petals

a yellow hole that follows Fibonacci
hinting a hidden march into infinity.

Every year, so much effort as if this
flower plots to become the sun,

outlive all stars, defy death itself,
as Van Gogh knew. The coup fails

every time only to return. As long
as it returns, we have hope and art.

Dishwasher Revelation

Damascus is reached in the apartment.

Call me pathetic,
but I think that if I can fill the dishwasher,
run it and empty it on one afternoon,
it's a victory.

I've stolen back time
from the consuming Domestic God,
time I can use tomorrow
not loading and emptying.

I can use it to devise
an amazing new poem, so good
it gets a prize,
or perhaps I will become Buddha

and realize that every desire
is a distraction from the truth.

Buddha never worried about dishes,
poetry submissions,
the dishes,
buying
back

time.

Witness

In a small slap of water
stands a hunched great blue heron

facing east, down the mostly empty irrigation canal,
feathers shivered by a wind,

or perhaps my worry
that this is all that is left

and the only thing to do
is to stand and witness.

Cicada Concert in Lucca

Atop the Medieval walls of Lucca,
where two parallel rows of flaking

chestnut trees defy explanation
and architecture, cicadas haze July's

air with their mating music. No
one else seems to notice; being

infused with familiarity, the daily
grind of sun on stone, they are tone-

deaf. As a tourist it's easy to think
we are the only ones marveling.

The cicadas have all summer,
we tourists have just today.

Why not sing and make poetry
to be heard and so briefly free.

Song from 'Landscape in the Riesengebirge,' by C.D. Friedrich

In Friedrich's lifetime the scale changed.
We refused to be gathered and humbled,
to know the beauty in being smaller,
to honor that which towers around us
and rises to the blurring heights that few
can see—the faint Unfathomable Above.
Is all that emptiness heartache or hope?
Answer: our mineral ambitions cropped
the peaks and turned the painting upside
down so that the tiny house of Man's god,
Mankind's monument to collective hope,
is atop the falling troughs of mountains
that point into the earth, the hollowed,
poisoned soil and all the darkness below.

At Belknap Hot Springs

This evening in the hot springs pool
murmurs of English, Russian, Spanish
spool up into the steam shifting shapes
of every animal imaginable, goddesses,
the winks and wishes of my wandering
mind, billowing into blurry nothingness
above the pool where frustrated stars
try to be seen between the glad steam
and the constellation of electric lights
streaming the fence that separates us
from the McKenzie River, the ceaseless,
force that pounds the evenings unseen.
I float and think it all a dream, a dream.

Return to Trees

I'm not saying

that in the six million years since
we stepped away from the trees
into the Savanna of civilization
we have not gained anything.

For all the hate speech, there's Hamlet,
for honking horns there's harmony.

But deep in our diaphragms
we know we've lost contact.

We feel it again, briefly,
when the wind shivers the trees
and we flutter with the feeling
that something missing

is back where we began.

Haiku

Ants don't know they walk
on a moving ball; can you
feel the Earth's orbit?

Barn swallow
skims and scans the sand for flies—
the Big Dipper

Bin of fish heads
asking mouths, shock-wide eyes—
the emptying sea.

In a building site
doe and fawn search for trees—
Memorial Day.

"?*!& move it"
shouted from a truck window . . .
The geese don't speed up

The top 1%
own two-thirds of the world's wealth.
Haiku? Who cares?

Notes

Pine Eagle: In Norse mythology Odin is the one-eyed All-Father, chief of the gods and god of poetry, amongst other things.

Songs From the Douglas Fir: In Greek mythology, Zeus is the chief of the Olympian gods of Olympus. The Titans were giant divine beings and enemies of the Olympians. Atlas was a Titan who was punished by Zeus and given the task of holding up the heavens.

At the Beach: In Hindu mythology, Brahma and Shiva are the Hindu gods of creation and destruction, respectively.

On New Year's Eve: In Taoism, the 'Ten Thousand Forms' refers to all of existence in its many forms.

Why Not the Cherry Tree: In Norse mythology Midgard is the realm of us humans, created from the body of the first giant, Ymir.

On Hearing 'River Snow' by Liu Zongyuan Recited in Chinese: 'River Snow' is a famous poem by Liu Zongyuan (773–819 A.D.) that conveys both literal and spiritual meaning.

Ukiyo-e in Oregon: Ukiyo-e is a type of wood block or painted art that flourished in Japan from the 17th to the 19th centuries. The words translate as 'picture of the floating world.' Hiroshige was one the most famous 19th-century masters of this art form.

Hummingbird Versus Cat: Huitzilopochtli was an Aztec sun and war god who was often represented by a hummingbird.

Song from 'Landscape in the Riesengebirge,' by C.D. Friedrich: Casper David Friedrich is one of Germany's most famous artists who specialized in romantic landscapes.

Postscript

I could write a list poem about the detritus of civilization we will grant our grandchildren in 2040—plastic beyond counting, radioactive residues, fossilized cities, billions of apology notes warping in dusty data servers, our corrupted DNA—but that would get too depressing. I want those secret oil company reports written in the 1970s about the cooking up of a future crisis to be wrong. No boardroom Nostrodamuses.

Instead, I will finish with the hope built into the etymology of 'apocalypse': revelation, uncover, disclose, reveal. May every child be given an empty Wunderkammer to fill with objects that delight and intrigue them. Hopefully, they can then grow up on and help preserve a planet that is, after all, our shared Wunderkammer.

About the Author

Matthew James Friday is a writer and teacher from England. He has an BA in Scriptwriting for Film and Television from Bournemouth University (UK) and an MA in Creative Writing from Goldsmith College, University of London. Matthew currently works as a grade-school teacher in an Oregon public school. He spent four years teaching in a public school in London and then moved to Germany to work in an international school, where he met his American wife, Jill. They then worked in China, Germany again and Switzerland. Matthew is also a professional storyteller for children.

As a poet, Matthew has had many poems published in US and international journals from all over the world. His chapbooks are *The Residents* (Finishing Line Press, 2024), *The Be-All and the End-All,* (Bottlecap Press, 2024), and *Strange Beauty* (Bottlecap Press, 2025). This book is his first full-length collection.

Since arriving in the US, at the height of the COVID pandemic, Matthew has become a father, ran half-marathons, bought a home, and learned to drive a car for the first time. He now lives with his wife and daughter in Bend, Oregon. The US feels like home now, especially as he has now achieved his dream of being a published poet.

More of his writing can be found at:
matthewfriday.weebly.com

www.ingramcontent.com/pod-product-compliance
Lightning Source LLC
LaVergne TN
LVHW090612110826
845146LV00001B/355

* 9 7 9 8 9 0 1 4 6 8 1 1 1 *